TO:

FROM:

DATE:

Published by Christian Art Publishers
PO Box 1599, Vereeniging, 1930, RSA

© 2015
First edition 2015

Cover designed by Christian Art Gifts

Images used under license from Shutterstock.com

Printed in China

ISBN 978-1-64272-465-3

21 22 23 24 25 26 27 28 29 30 – 12 11 10 9 8 7 6 5 4 3

WE HAVE THIS

HOPE

COLORING BOOK

CHRISTIAN ART
PUBLISHERS

LET THE SEA & everything in it shout HIS praise!

Psalm 98:7

Praise the Lord from the EARTH, you creatures of the OCEAN depths.

Psalm 148:7

LET YOUR *light* *Shine* BEFORE OTHERS.

MATTHEW 5:16

In high tide or low tide
God will be by your side.

When You Go THROUGH DEEP WATERS, I will be WITH You.

ISAIAH 43:2

FOOTPRINTS

ONE NIGHT I HAD A DREAM.

I WAS WALKING ALONG THE BEACH

WITH THE

LORD

I NOTICED TWO SETS OF

FOOTPRINTS

IN THE SAND.

ONE WAS MINE, AND ONE WAS THE LORD'S

...TO MY SURPRISE

I NOTICED THAT MANY TIMES ALONG THE PATH OF MY LIFE

THERE WAS ONLY ONE SET OF

FOOTPRINTS

THE LORD SAID:

"MY PRECIOUS CHILD

WHERE YOU SEE ONLY ONE SET OF

FOOTPRINTS

IT WAS THEN THAT

I CARRIED YOU."

THE LORD RESTORES MY SOUL.

PSALM 23:3

Hope
IN THE
Lord
Psalm 130:7

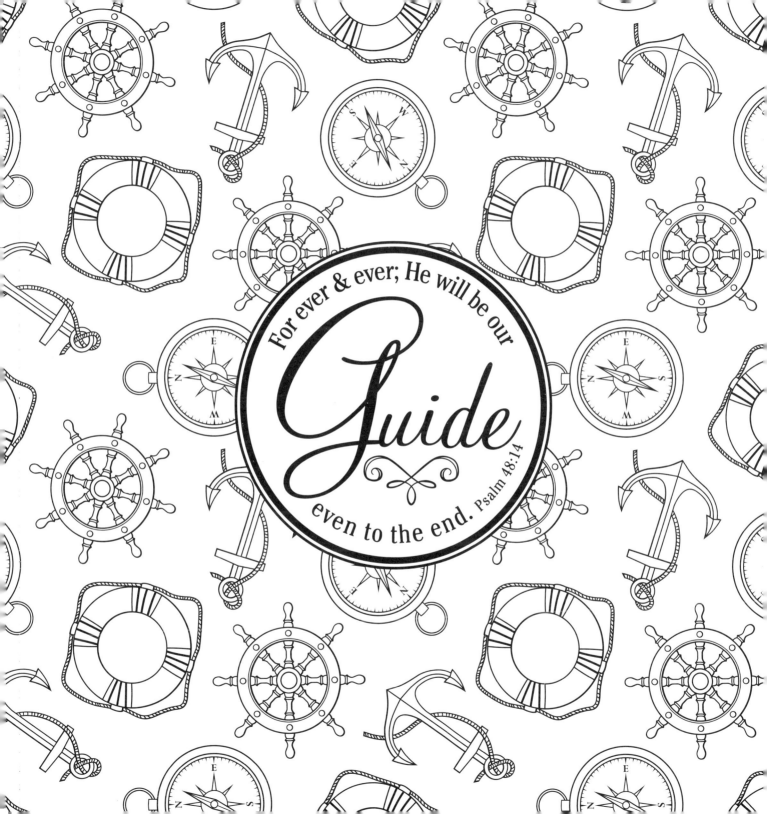

For ever & ever; He will be our *Guide* even to the end. Psalm 48:14

HE WHO DWELLS IN THE SHELTER OF THE MOST High WILL rest IN THE SHADOW OF THE ALMIGHTY

PSALM 91:1

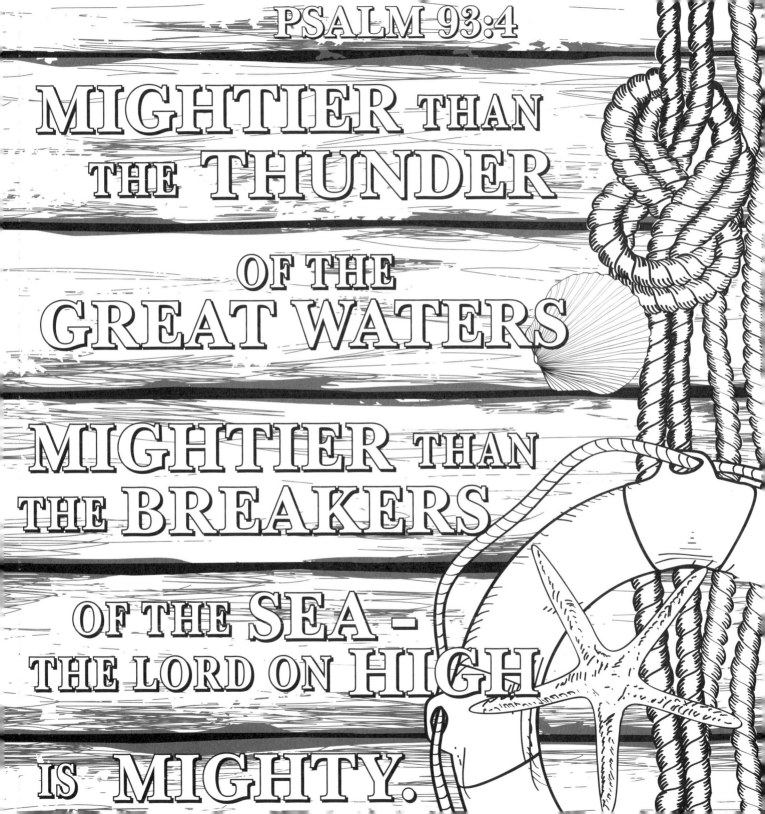

More than the grains of sand are His thoughts for you!

THE EARTH shall be filled with the KNOWLEDGE of the GLORY of the LORD as the WATERS cover the SEA.

HABAKKUK 2:14

BE STILL AND KNOW THAT I AM GOD

PSALM 46:10

THE LORD KEEPS WATCH OVER YOU

AS YOU COME AND GO,

BOTH NOW AND FOREVER. PSALM 121:8

FOLDING LINE

FOLDING LINE